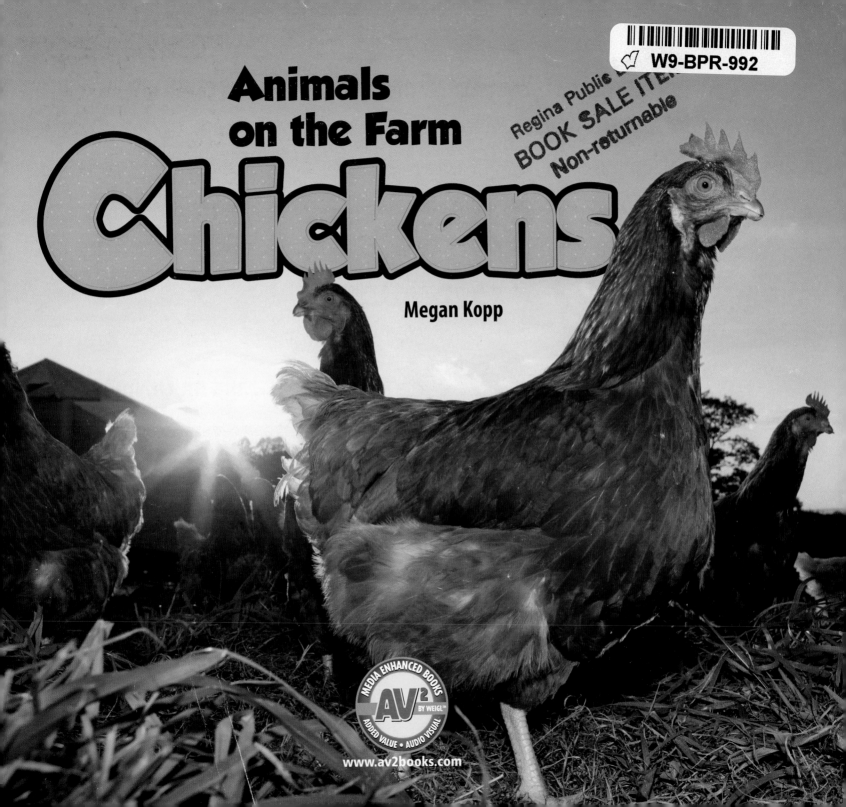

Animals on the Farm

Chickens

Megan Kopp

MEDIA ENHANCED BOOKS
AV2 BY WEIGL
ADDED VALUE • AUDIO VISUAL

www.av2books.com

AV² provides enriched content that supplements and complements this book. Weigl's AV² books strive to create inspired learning and engage young minds in a total learning experience.

Your AV² Media Enhanced books come alive with...

Go to **www.av2books.com**, and enter this book's unique code.

BOOK CODE

W812055

AV² by Weigl brings you media enhanced books that support active learning.

Audio
Listen to sections of the book read aloud.

Video
Watch informative video clips.

Embedded Weblinks
Gain additional information for research.

Try This!
Complete activities and hands-on experiments.

Key Words
Study vocabulary, and complete a matching word activity.

Quizzes
Test your knowledge.

Slide Show
View images and captions, and prepare a presentation.

... and much, much more!

Published by AV² by Weigl.
350 5th Avenue, 59th Floor
New York, NY 10118
Website: www.av2books.com   www.weigl.com

Library of Congress Cataloging-in-Publication Data

Kopp, Megan.
  Chickens / Megan Kopp.
      p. cm. -- (Animals on the farm)
  Includes index.
  ISBN 978-1-61913-275-7 (hard cover : alk. paper) -- ISBN 978-1-61913-279-5 (soft cover : alk. paper)
  1. Chickens--Juvenile literature. I. Title.
  SF487.5.K67 2013
  636.5--dc23
                              2011049122

Printed in the United States of America in North Mankato, Minnesota
1 2 3 4 5 6 7 8 9 0 16 15 14 13 12

022012
WEP020212

Project Coordinator: Aaron Carr   Art Director: Terry Paulhus

Weigl acknowledges Getty Images as the primary image supplier for this title.

Animals
on the Farm
Chickens

CONTENTS

4

I am a small farm animal.
Farmers keep me
for my eggs and for food.

I am a bird. I have feathers over most of my body.

I have wings, but I do not fly.
I walk around the farm.

9

I have red skin on my head.
It is called a comb.

I scratch the ground
to look for food.
I like to eat seeds and bugs.

13

I make a "clucking" sound
to talk with other chickens.
Male chickens "crow."

I live in a group
of many chickens.
If I am the top chicken,
I get to eat first.

I lay eggs and sit on them to keep them warm.

My chicks hatch from these eggs.

My chicks learn to walk just hours after they hatch. They can find food on their own.

CHICKEN FACTS

These pages provide more detail about the interesting facts found in the book. They are intended to be used by adults as a learning support to help young readers round out their knowledge of each animal featured in the Animals on the Farm series.

Pages 4–5

Farmers keep chickens for their eggs. Most farmers raise chickens for eggs and meat. These chickens are called poultry. On farms, chickens are kept in small buildings called coops. Coops have an attached area called a run where the chickens can walk around. Coops provide nesting space and protection from predators.

Pages 6–7

Chickens are birds. Chickens are a type of bird, similar to robins and owls. A chicken's feathers are called plumage. Chicken feathers can be many colors. They can be white, gray, yellow, blue, red, brown, or black. Their feathers can also be mottled, or spotted.

Pages 8–9

Chickens have wings, but they cannot fly. Farm chickens have heavy bodies and short wings. Their wings are not large enough to lift their heavy bodies into the air for more than a few seconds. Some chickens can fly short distances, but they still spend much of their time walking around in search of food on the ground.

Pages 10–11

Chickens have red skin on their heads. Chickens have a ridge of red skin called a comb on top of their heads. They also have two wrinkly folds of skin called wattles hanging below their chins. The wattle and comb help cool chickens in hot weather. Male chickens, called roosters, have larger combs than female chickens, or hens.

Chickens scratch the ground to look for food. Chickens have four-toed feet with sharp claws on each toe. They search for food in the dirt by scratching with their claws and pecking with their beaks. Chickens eat insects, seeds, fruit, snails, and worms. A part of a chicken's stomach called a gizzard holds rocks that grind its food.

Chickens talk by clucking, crowing, or peeping. When a chick is ready to hatch from its egg, it peeps. The hen hears this sound and starts to cluck, telling the chick to break the shell. Peeping and clucking are how chicks and hens communicate with each other. Roosters crow to warn other roosters and predators to stay away.

Chickens like to be with other chickens. Chickens are social animals. They can recognize each other by facial features. Chickens have a pecking order within their flocks. Chickens that are on the top of the pecking order are the leaders. They have first access to food and nests.

Chickens lay eggs. Their chicks hatch from the eggs. Hens start laying eggs between 18 and 22 weeks of age. Hens can lay one egg each day for up to 30 days. A hen will sit on her egg for 21 days to keep it warm. Hens use their beaks to turn their eggs over regularly. They do this to ensure the chick does not stick to the side of the egg.

Chicks can walk and find their own food right after hatching. When they are ready to hatch, chicks peck their way out of their eggshell. Newly hatched chicks do not have adult feathers. They are covered with soft, fuzzy feathers called down. Chicks can walk a few hours after hatching. They scratch and peck for food without any help.

WORD LIST

Research has shown that as much as 65 percent of all written material published in English is made up of 300 words. These 300 words cannot be taught using pictures or learned by sounding them out. They must be recognized by sight. This book contains 54 common sight words to help young readers improve their reading fluency and comprehension. This book also teaches young readers several important content words. These words are paired with pictures to aid in learning and improve understanding.

Page	Sight Words First Appearance
5	a, am, and, animal, farm, food, for, I, keep, me, my, small
6	have, most, of, over
8	around, but, do, not, the, walk
11	head, is, it, on
13	eat, like, look, to
15	make, other, sound, talk, with
17	first, get, group, if, in, live, many, of
18	them
19	from, these
20	after, can, find, just, learn, own, their, they

Page	Content Words First Appearance
5	eggs, farmers
6	bird, body, feathers
8	wings
11	comb, skin
13	bugs, ground, seeds
15	chickens
19	chicks
20	hours